Dear Parents and Educators,

Welcome to Penguin Young Readers! As parents and educators, you know that each child develops at his or her own pace—in terms of speech, critical thinking, and, of course, reading. Penguin Young Readers recognizes this fact. As a result, each Penguin Young Readers book is assigned a traditional easy-to-read level (1–4) as well as a Guided Reading Level (A–P). Both of these systems will help you choose the right book for your child. Please refer to the back of each book for specific leveling information. Penguin Young Readers features esteemed authors and illustrators, stories about favorite characters, fascinating nonfiction, and more!

Kit-Kit-Kittens

LEVEL **2**

GUIDED READING LEVEL **I**

This book is perfect for a **Progressing Reader** who:
- can figure out unknown words by using picture and context clues;
- can recognize beginning, middle, and ending sounds;
- can make and confirm predictions about what will happen in the text; and
- can distinguish between fiction and nonfiction.

Here are some **activities** you can do during and after reading this book:
- Nonfiction: Nonfiction books deal with facts and events that are real. Talk about the elements of nonfiction. On a separate piece of paper, write down the facts you learned about kittens from this book.
- Sight Words: Sight words are frequently used words that readers know just by looking at them. These words are not "sounded out" or "decoded"; rather they are known instantly, on sight. Knowing these words helps children become efficient and smooth readers. As you are reading or rereading the story, have the child point out the sight words.

every	how	of	there
give	just	over	walk
her	may	take	when

Remember, sharing the love of reading with a child is the best gift you can give!

—Bonnie Bader, EdM
  Penguin Young Readers program

*Penguin Young Readers are leveled by independent reviewers applying the standards developed by Irene Fountas and Gay Su Pinnell in *Matching Books to Readers: Using Leveled Books in Guided Reading*, Heinemann, 1999.

To Bailey, who thinks she is a kitten!—BB

PENGUIN YOUNG READERS
Published by the Penguin Group
Penguin Group (USA) LLC, 375 Hudson Street, New York, New York 10014, USA

USA | Canada | UK | Ireland | Australia | New Zealand | India | South Africa | China

penguin.com
A Penguin Random House Company

Photo credits: cover, title page: © GK Hart/Vikki Hart/Stone/Getty Images; page 4: © Thinkstock/Dixi;
page 5: © Thinkstock/GrishaL; page 6, page 7, page 14 (bottom), page 22 (middle): © Thinkstock/
EEI_Tony; page 8: © Hulya Ozkok/Getty Images; page 9: © Thinkstock/Khorzhevska; page 10 (top),
page 13 (top), page 14 (top), page 18: © Thinkstock/GlobalP; page 10 (bottom): © Thinkstock/Rumo;
page 11 (top): © Thinkstock/Yulia Saponova, page 11 (bottom): © Thinkstock/gabes1976; page 12: ©
Thinkstock/Photosampler; page 13 (bottom): © Thinkstock/Eric IsselTe; page 15: © Benjamin Torode/
Getty Images; page 16: © Sebastian Pfuetze/Getty Images; page 17: © Thinkstock/Ferenc Szelepcsenyi;
page 19: © Thinkstock/annadarzy; page 20: © Thinkstock/irin717; page 21: © Thinkstock/Andrejs
Pidiass; page 22 (top): © Jeffrey Sylvester/Getty Images; page 22 (bottom): © Thinkstock/Kyoungil
Jeon; page 23: © Thinkstock/Magone; page 24: © perets/Getty Images; page 25: © Thinkstock/
orelphoto; page 26 (top): © Thinkstock/Yanikap; page 26 (bottom): © Thinkstock/sergoua; page 27: ©
Thinkstock/Norman Chan; page 28: © Thinkstock/bloodua; page 29: © Steve Lyne/Getty Images; page
30 (right): © Thinkstock/Cherry-Merry; page 30 (left): © Thinkstock/heatheralvis; page 31 (top): ©
Thinkstock/fantom_rd ; page 31 (bottom): © Thinkstock/Paffy69; page 32: © Thinkstock/fuse.

Library of Congress Cataloging-in-Publication Data is available.

ISBN 978-0-448-48443-3 (pbk)   10 9 8 7 6 5 4 3 2 1
ISBN 978-0-448-48444-0 (hc)   10 9 8 7 6 5 4 3 2 1

Kit-Kit-Kittens

by Bonnie Bader

Penguin Young Readers
An Imprint of Penguin Group (USA) LLC

Kit.

Kit.

Kittens!

Kittens run.

Kittens leap.

Kittens curl up to sleep.

Kittens pounce.

Kittens purr.

Kittens love to lick their fur.

Kittens make the best pets.

It is fun to get a new kitten.

But kittens can be a lot of work.

A grown-up can show you how to take care of your kitten.

Do not grab your kitten.

Gently pick her up.

Pet her softly.

You can teach your kitten
many things.

First, she must learn her name.

Call her name often.

Say it over and over when you are

playing with her.

You can teach your kitten rules.

No biting.

No scratching.

Sometimes your kitten will behave badly.

Do not yell if your kitten is bad.

She will not understand.

You can walk away.

Or you can gently tell her no.

If your kitten is good, give her a treat!

It is important to feed your kitten good food.

You can buy food at the pet store.

Young kittens need to be fed
three to four times a day.
At six months,
your kitten can be fed
two times a day.

You can teach your kitten where
to go to the bathroom.

Set up a box for your kitten.

Make sure to clean the box
every day.

Your kitten needs to go to the

doctor just like you do!

Kittens love to play.

You can take your kitten outside.

But be careful.

Your kitten can run away fast.

Take her outside in her carrier

or on a leash.

Kittens also love to sleep.

Nap time!

Kittens can sleep up to

16 hours a day.

Kittens can clean themselves.

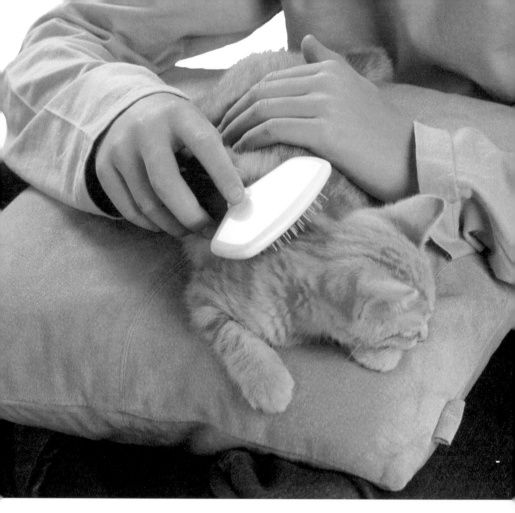

But you should clean

your kitten, too.

Brush her with a soft brush.

Look for little bugs

that may be in her fur.

There are many things a kitten
can do.

But most of all,

your kitten will love you!